Person of Colour

Maya Jina

BookLeaf Publishing

India | USA | UK

Presentation by *BookLeaf Publishing*

Web: www.bookleafpub.com

E-mail: info@bookleafpub.com

ISBN : 9789357448772

First edition 2021

DEDICATION

To all the people out there that are struggling to find the colour in life, I hope this helps you find it.

ACKNOWLEDGEMENT

I'd like to thank all the important people in my life who make my world as colourful as it is.

Thank you to my parents for supporting me through anything and making each day a little brighter.

Thank you to my teacher, Ms. Lora, for being the reason that I am now a published author. You have helped me develop my voice as a writer and create a collection that I can be proud of.

Thank you to Aarushi, Ayana, Ranya, Madison, Kaylin and Tanisha, who read through my poems at the most random times and gave me enough confidence in my writing to not delete every word that I wrote.

Thank you to all my other friends, especially Carolina, Evelyn, and Jack, for unknowingly setting me on many writing sprees when I was lacking inspiration (seriously, you guys never fail to entertain).

Ruby Red

Red is for unity
Like gemstones on a string
Each sparkling ruby
Has a talent to bring
Together they glisten,
(they shine brighter that way)

Like the blood in our veins
(it's the same, it's all red)
It follows us daily
A lingering thought in our heads.

No matter our flaws
Our friends or our foes
We are all united under an umbrella of red.

Orange

Orange is a shirt
that stands for something more.
Reconciliation. Reflection.
And above all, remorse.

Orange is our history,
Too dark for us to face.
A tornado around us
Stirring up feelings of shame.

Orange is the lies
(oh there are so many lies)
It's the injustice, unfairness,
Manipulation and despise.

Orange is the hatred,
Discrimination and tragedy.
The world imploding
into a supernova of destruction.

Orange is the wrongs of the past
And the lessons of the present
It's the awareness that is growing
To combat the deep and ugly truth.

Orange is the setbacks
And the deep-rooted issues
The daily struggle
For the progress still being made.

Cyber Yellow

Bright and bubbly,
a smile greets me each morning.
A friend who's so lively,
I can't help but grin back.
Her energy is infectious,
hugging me like a warm blanket
one I wish I could stay wrapped up in forever.

But like the sun has to set,
all things eventually end.
And so I sit here
on a cold moonlit night
waiting for the sun to rise
and the warmth of yellow to come back.

Leaf Green

Forests.
Mountains.
Mystery.
Green is you
And green is me.
Green is life,
The world itself.
A dark pigment
Leafy and vibrant.

Aquamarine

Bright and luminescent
like a mystical glowing algae
a forbidden coral
hidden deep beneath the waves
eternally encased in my heart.

Cotton Candy Blue

the soft fluffy blue
a melt-in-your-mouth treat
the sweetness brings me back
to my days of being a kid
concerts and Calaway
the times when I was carefree
a sticky sugary confection
which always got all over me
cotton candy always brought a smile to my face
(a blue smile - but a smile nonetheless)
||
||
||

Ocean Blue

Blue is the source of my nerves,
the haunting colour as bold as the deep sea.
Its waves wash over me;
cold and unwelcome,
inviting the anxiety to creep even farther up the
shore.
My stomach churns
but I swallow my nerves
and like water trickling down my throat
they slowly fade away.
The waves die down,
the foamy white caps fizzle out as the water
evaporates
just like the beads of sweat on my face.
The nerves are now gone
like the retreating tide,
washing away to reveal the sand underneath.

My confidence returns,
standing tall like a tsunami.

Wythe Blue

A dull mint,
solid and stable.
A surface to stare at
as the voices drone on.
The colour is nothing special
-a pale grey with a hint of blue -
but I see it so often
it barely registers in my mind.

Purple

My hightop Vans
A symbol for good luck
A sign of comfort
A bearer of smiles

Purple is bright
Mysterious and joyful
An exotic colour
Wild
And full of creativity.
(purple is just like me)

Violet

She was my ray of light,
always guiding me along.
Her smile shone so bright,
With a joy that could never vanquish.

And yet it did.

Just like the violets in the field,
their soft petals bloomed in spring
but wilted and withered away in the winter.
It seemed as though her summer lasted forever,
never giving in to the chills of fall.
But the seasons must pass
and her winter came too.
The cold washed the warmth away,
the flowers left to die.
And when summer came,
they no longer littered the lawn.
Gone were the violets,
the pale purples a forgotten memory,
a symbol dead in her world.

The smile on her face,
I wish it had stayed.

Teal & Lavender

Comfort.
Chaos.
Calm and consoling.

Pale shades that fill the space.
the curtains,
the lampshade,
the colours of my room
that I see first thing each morning
and make me smile.

Bubblegum Pink

The burst of bubblegum
The pop in my ears
The build-up of pressure
Before an explosion of tears.

It's hard to let it out;
To let the emotions flow
To let my walls break down
And my true feelings show

But the weight never fades
It stays there -
Sticky like bubblegum -
And the stress only ever shrinks
When I spit it all out;
A spew of words and feelings
And a waterfall of tears.

(drip drop)
(drip drop)
They finally spill out.

Blue vs Pink

Baby blue. Pastel pink.
He. She.
Husband. Wife.
Fierce. Frail.
Pragmatic. Emotional.
A money maker. A housekeeper.
A businessman. A child-bearer.
A knight in shining armour. A damsel in
distress.
As a man he is strong, but as a woman I am
weak.
I have no free will,
I am to carry out his.
My name is my father's,
My will is his too.
I am a daughter, a sister, a maid.
Yet the men get the titles,
The prizes and praise.

Chocolate Brown

The scent of chocolate chip cookies
Fresh off the tray
A constant comfort always lingering in the air.
My mother's baking,
Sweet treats from my youth
The warm brown of Dairy Milk
Her favourite kind of chocolate

The deep brown of the dinner table
The home of fresh meals
Made with love
Prepared with care.

Brown is belonging;
My loving family.

Beige

Ongoing prairies,
rolling hills of endless crop.
A dull, counterfeit gold
that feels as fake as Her.

That overzealous smile,
(it's sickening to look at)
the way she toys with others;
the world holds little significance next to her.

Hearts get crushed
People turn to puppets.

I've lost my mind, my soul, my being
to that of her cruel hands.

Gold

Some say gold speaks to victory,
to success and to the rich.
But to me, it's hard work,
perseverance,
and determination.
Gold is the path I follow
with friends and family by my side.
The persistence and patience
until I finally get it right.
Gold is a medal,
a reward after a long struggle
the prize for after you've endured the pain
and made it through to the end.

Gold is my pride.
Gold is my conviction.

Noir

Just like the stars, her eyes will never glow,
Instead, they are the darkness of the night.
Her face can not be made to look like snow
Her mangled mane is not compared to light.
The darkness is not beautiful they say
But they forget the fairness of the dark.
Without the black, there is no light, no day.
The shadows let you see the fire spark.
The earth is dull yet nature we admire
The coal lacks sparkle, glisten it does not
But from it come the diamonds we desire.
From oysters come pearls which after are
sought.

The shade is no less stunning than the sun
Dark features make just as fair a person.

Black

In darkness I find excitement
At the prospect of the unknown.

In the night sky, I find endless adventure
Searching for faraway stars.

In the blank screen, I find questions to ask
An infinite void of information.

In the inky text, I find a story to be told
A fictional world to which I can escape.

Black is my curiosity
Boundless and untamed
It reaches out like a shadow
Finding meaning in the void.

Grey

My insides churn
like the grey sky above,
a dark inclement heaven
mere minutes from

                            coming

                                  crashing

                                 down.

my mind is

s   a   t   r   d
   c   t   e   e

my body is n u m b

Tears
      stream
          down
              my
                 face
(and god, I wish I knew why)

White

People are shouting
But to me, it's all white noise
Sounds pass right through me;
I've heard them all before
So I sit and ignore it,
just like I'm being ignored.

My teammates all chatter,
But I am shut out,
Left on my own
to try and figure it all out.

The adults watch in pity
Unsure of what to do
And I welcome the silence,
As something I'm used to.

It shouldn't be this way, I think,
A child left here all alone.
I've never felt more isolated
than when I am out on the ice

White is my silence,
The ice on which my eyes rest.
The colour of my jersey

And our team crest.

Watching the clock tick,
waiting for the hour to pass by.
No one notices me disappear,
And there are no lively shouts of goodbye.

Everyone else gets it:
The attention, the friendships.
But not me.
(Never me)

I'm the snow on the ground
That gets trampled and stepped on,
But never really, truly looked upon.

I sit in silence
Because white is my setting
From which I watch the world around me
Wondering why it has to be so cruel.

Rainbow

Rainbow is for the mental breakdowns
And the flashing LEDs
At 6:50pm on a Wednesday evening
(ROYGBIV, they light up my room)

Rainbow is for community
One shunned from society
Brought together by our differences
(rainbow is my pride)

Rainbow is the world around me
Colours both bright and dull
Representing both the good and bad
The light and the dark
My world and yours.
(colour shapes my world)

www.ingramcontent.com/pod-product-compliance
Lightning Source LLC
LaVergne TN
LVHW050504210726

843509LV00015BA/2979